INSIDE GUIDES

ANIMAL REPRODUCTION

Written by
DAVID BURNIE

DK PUBLISHING, INC.

A DK PUBLISHING BOOK

Editor Julie Ferris

Senior art editor Jill Plank

DTP designer Nicola Studdart

Senior managing editor Gillian Denton

Senior managing art editor Julia Harris

US editors William Lach, Kristin Ward

Picture research Kate Duncan

Production Charlotte Traill

Photography Geoff Brightling

Modelmakers Peter Minister Model FX,

Dave Morgan, Chris Reynolds and the BBC team,

and Gary and Lissi Staab

Empid flies
mating

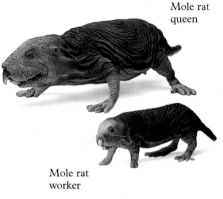

Mole rat
queen

Mole rat
worker

Development inside a
chicken's egg

First American Edition, 1998

2 4 6 8 10 9 7 5 3 1

Published in the United States by
DK Publishing, Inc.
95 Madison Avenue,
New York, NY 10016

Visit us on the
World Wide Web at http://www.dk.com

Copyright © 1998
Dorling Kindersley Limited,
London

Library of Congress Cataloging-in-Publication Data
p. cm. – (An inside guide)
Summary: Text and more than 250 annotated, colored
photographs depict how a variety of animals clone
themselves asexually or create unique offspring with
at least one other parent.
ISBN 0-7894-2901-2
1. Reproduction – Juvenile literature.
2. Animals – Juvenile literature.
[1. Reproduction. 2. Animals.]
I. Dk Publishing, Inc. II. Series: Inside guides.
QP251.5.A54 1998
573.6–dc21

Reproduced in Italy by
GRB Editrice S.r.l., Verona
Printed in Singapore by Toppan

Cross section
of a tapeworm
showing the
reproductive
organs

Contents

Juvenile aphids

Mouthbrooding cichlid expelling young

What is reproduction?

Reproduction is the most important feature of living things. Without it, they would slowly die out, and nothing would be left to take their place. Reproduction allows different species to thrive and spread, and it allows living things to pass on their characteristics. In the animal world, reproduction works in many different ways. Some animals can reproduce entirely on their own, while others need a partner of the opposite sex or one that is both sexes at once. Many animals lay eggs, others give birth to live young, and some simply split in half. The tiniest animals can produce hundreds of offspring in the space of a few weeks, but the largest – such as elephants and whales – often take years to raise a single baby.

In at the finish
Only about one percent of sperm come within striking distance of the egg cell.

Feathers dry out soon after hatching

Jacket of jelly
A jelly-like layer called the zona pellucida surrounds the egg cell.

Into the outside world
As this baby ostrich pecks its way out of its egg, it looks as though it is just starting life. But like most other animals, its life actually begins at the moment of fertilization, when a sperm and egg cell join together.

Delivering genes
The head of a sperm cell contains a set of the father's genes.

Awesome odds
Over 500 million sperm cells may make their way toward the egg cell, but only one will fertilize it.

Young hydra budding from parent

Population explosion
In the course of their short lives, female blowflies can lay over 600 eggs. Animals that breed quickly have many predators that keep their numbers in check, so there is no chance of flies overrunning the earth.

On the move
Sperm cells swim toward the egg cell by wriggling their tails.

Lone parent
Some animals, such as this hydra, can reproduce without having to find a mate. A hydra grows buds that turn into new animals. Other lone parents can produce young from eggs that develop without being fertilized.

Chemical receptors
The zona pellucida contains chemicals that react with sperm cells.

Cell membrane
A thin inner membrane surrounds the egg cell.

Stored away
The egg cell's nucleus contains a set of the mother's genes.

Contact
The first sperm to reach the egg enters the zona pellucida. The surface suddenly changes to stop any other sperm from getting in.

Left behind
The sperm's head is absorbed into the egg cell, but its tail is left outside.

Starting out
The mother's and father's genes are brought together inside a new nucleus.

Development
Once fertilization has occurred, the egg cell starts to divide.

A new life begins

For most animals, life begins at the moment of fertilization. This takes place when a male sperm cell finds its way to a female egg cell and then works its way inside. Once the genes from both cells have fused together, the fertilized cell can develop into a complete new animal. In some animals, sperm and eggs meet up outside the parents' bodies, but in mammal reproduction, fertilization occurs inside the female's reproductive system.

Long childhood
An elephant does not breed until it is about 15 years old.

Small beginnings
Despite weighing nearly half a ton, this baby elephant started life in the same way as a baby mouse – from a single fertilized egg. A fertilized egg cell contains genes from the father and the mother, so the young animal inherits a mixture of features from both its parents.

Single parents

Microscopic protozoan dividing in two

For small freshwater animals called hydras, reproduction is a simple matter. An adult hydra grows small "buds" on the side of its body, and each of these slowly turns into a complete new animal. "Budding" is an example of asexual reproduction – a way of making young that involves just one parent. This kind of reproduction can be quick and easy, but it does have one important disadvantage. Unlike sexual reproduction, it always produces young identical to the parent, and any weak points the parent had are duplicated in the young. Hydras have a way around this problem. Like aphids (pp. 30–31), they normally use asexual reproduction when there is plenty of food and conditions for survival are good, but switch to sexual reproduction when times become harder.

Collecting a meal
The hydra uses its ring of tentacles to pull food toward its mouth.

Hollow insides
A hydra's body is like a hollow tube. It is open at the mouth but usually sealed at the base.

Rotifers
Microscopic rotifers are among the world's smallest animals. They live in water and damp places, and most of them are less than 0.02 in (0.5 mm) long. One of the reasons for their success is that the females can reproduce rapidly without having to mate. In many species, males have never been found.

Hydras are about 0.2 in (5 mm) long

Digesting food
Cells lining the digestive cavity produce chemicals that break down the hydra's food.

Attached
Hydras attach their base to underwater plants.

Living scales
Like their relatives aphids (pp. 30–31), scale insects often reproduce without having to mate. Their eggs develop into young without being fertilized. Female scale insects live by sucking sap from plants and hardly look like insects at all. They spend their adult lives fastened to plants and are protected by a hard scalelike shield. Male scale insects are much smaller. Unlike the females, they have wings.

Paralyzed prey
This young water flea has been immobilized by stinging cells on the hydra's tentacles.

Deadly stings
Each tentacle is armed with dozens of stinging cells, or nematocysts.

Changing shape
A hydra can pull in its tentacles or spread them wide to catch food.

Second option
When hydras reproduce sexually, they make both egg and sperm cells. This bump is an ovary – an organ that will produce a single egg.

Tentacular ring
Hydras usually have five or six tentacles, arranged in a ring around their mouths.

Dividing bacterium
This bacterium, a microscopic organism, is about to divide in two, producing two new cells. In good conditions, bacteria can divide every 20 minutes, which means that a single bacterium can quickly produce many millions of offspring. This kind of rapid reproduction makes some bacteria quite dangerous, because they can rapidly spread through food or the body.

No escape
This tiny worm is being drawn inside the hydra's body, where it will be digested.

Budding baby
Although they are still fastened together, this parent hydra and its young are two separate animals. At first, the young hydra shares food that its parent has caught, because its digestive cavity is connected to its parent's. However, as its tentacles develop, it starts to catch food for itself. The young hydra has just seized a meal, and it will soon be ready to take up life on its own.

Moving along
Hydras can move by taking steps with their tentacles. In emergencies, they can escape from danger in a series of slow-motion somersaults.

Ready for action
A hydra's tentacles are sensitive to touch and also to chemicals produced by passing animals.

Torn in two
Sea anemones are close relatives of hydras. Although most produce young by sexual reproduction, some can also reproduce asexually by tearing themselves in two. This sea anemone is partway through the process.

Slow separation
Flatworms, or planarians, sometimes reproduce asexually simply by leaving part of themselves behind. The flatworm's body starts to narrow, and the rear part eventually pulls itself away. The rear grows a new head, while the front of the worm grows a new tail. These two flatworms have narrowed bodies, and they will soon divide in this way.

Courting couples

Male stickleback fish displaying bright red courting colors

In the animal world, it is usually the male's job to attract a partner. Males do this by using special courtship displays. These displays show that the male is strong and healthy, and that he belongs to the right species. If a female is sufficiently impressed by a male's courtship display, she will allow him to approach her and mate. Courtship displays vary enormously between different animals. Some attract attention through noises, while others show off eyecatching body parts.

Changing color
The claw often becomes brightly colored in the breeding season.

This fiddler crab's claw is outstretched at the start.

The male then raises its giant claw as high as it can.

The claw quickly drops back to rest in front of the crab.

The fiddler crab rests for a while before the display begins again.

All puffed up
Male frigate birds attract females with the help of an inflatable throat pouch that looks like a red balloon. During the breeding season, each male looks for a suitable nest site and puffs up his pouch as females fly overhead.

Signals on the shore
Fiddler crabs live in the mud of mangrove swamps. At low tide, they come out of their burrows, and the males signal to females by waving a single giant claw. Each kind of fiddler crab uses a different sequence of movements, so females are always attracted to the right species of mate. Although fiddler crabs are tiny, the male's display is easy to see across the flat mud.

Ready to run
Agile legs help the crab speed into its burrow at the first sign of danger.

Pulling power
Males with the biggest claws attract the most females.

Either side
The giant claw can be either on the left or the right.

Clumsy claw
The giant claw is too big to be used for feeding. It is only used for signaling.

Animal attraction
Some male birds, like this ruff, gather together during the breeding season and display in special courtship arenas called leks. Females watch as the males perform the displays, and then they mate with whichever one impresses them the most.

Weight lifters
Extra-large muscles raise the claw and open and close the pincers. The crab often rests the claw in the mud.

Doubled up
This frog has a pair of vocal sacs. Some frogs have a single vocal sac underneath their throats.

Calling with a croak

For frogs, sound plays an important part in courtship. Many species, including these tungara frogs from Central and South America, have special vocal sacs that help to amplify their calls. Frogs usually call at night, when it is harder for predators to track them down. However, if frogs do hear anything suspicious, they immediately stop calling and disappear under the water.

Air-filled float
The vocal sac helps the frog to keep its head above water.

Surface call
The frog floats at the water surface as it calls.

Smelly scent
Male cats have glands that produce a powerful scent.

Cat courtship

In the cat world, courtship can be a slow and sometimes noisy business. The male uses scent to mark his territory, and he courts females by making noises that are very unappealing to human ears.

Keen eyesight
Stalked eyes give the crab a good view of its rivals and approaching enemies.

Body is covered by a hard case

Calming moments
For cats, grooming is often a way of defusing tension.

Snapping shut
The claw muscles can pull the pincers shut.

Fit for feeding
The crab uses its small claw to pick up particles of food from the mud.

13

All in one

When adult slugs or snails get together to breed, they do not have to worry about finding a partner of the opposite sex. This is because most slugs and snails are both male and female at the same time, which means any two adults can mate. After a long and slimy courtship, each animal fertilizes its partner, and both partners then slither away to lay a batch of eggs. Animals that are both male and female are called hermaphrodites. They include a wide variety of invertebrates (animals without backbones) but only a few vertebrates. As well as true hermaphrodites, the animal world also includes species that mix up the sexes in a different way. These animals start adult life as one sex and then slowly change into the other.

Love dart

Snail courtship really gets moving when one of the snails fires a "love dart" into its partner. The love dart is made of a chalky substance, and it is sharp enough to penetrate its partner's skin. This dart has fallen to the ground.

Hermaphrodite fish

Many fish change sex as they get older, but the brightly striped comber is one of the few species that is a true hermaphrodite. Unlike a slug or snail, the comber can fertilize its own eggs, which means that it does not have to find a partner in order to breed.

Give and take

When snails mate, each one unfolds its penis and inserts it into its partner. The two snails remain locked together for up to six hours, while they each deliver and receive a package of sperm called a spermatophore. After mating, these slowly break open, and the sperm fertilizes each snail's eggs.

Joining the pile

Slipper limpets fasten themselves to one another's shells and live in piles of up to nine animals. The oldest limpets, at the bottom of the pile, are always female. All limpets start out as male, but gradually turn into females when more limpets join the pile.

Hanging by a thread

When great gray slugs are ready to mate, they climb up a wall or a tree and then lower themselves into midair on a thread of slime. Once upside down, they lower their penises, which unfold into a shape like an umbrella. After mating, the two slugs crawl back up the thread, eating it as they go.

Penises twined together

Ovotestis produces both eggs and sperms

Laying eggs

Garden snails lay their eggs in early summer, when the ground is warm but damp. Each snail digs a shallow pit in some loose earth, and then drops about 50 pearly eggs into the hole. The eggs hatch into tiny snails with transparent shells, then they crawl up to the surface.

Mucus glands
These glands produce slime that is used when the snails mate.

Sperm storage
A sperm package is stored in this chamber after it is received from the other snail. The package's wrapping dissolves after several days.

Dart sac
This muscular chamber contains the snail's dart, which is fired at the start of courtship.

Flagellum
This whiplike tube makes the substances that form the wrapping of the sperm package.

Retractor muscle

Penis
When mating is over, the snail's penis is pulled back into its body by a special retractor muscle.

Muscular foot

Albumen gland
This forms a jelly-like substance that coats the snail's eggs. It helps to stop them drying out.

Reproductive duct
This carries sperm from an organ called the ovotestis and also stores the eggs.

Close encounters

For an animal to breed, sperm cells must meet up with egg cells so that the egg cells can be fertilized. In water most animals use external fertilization. They simply release their eggs and sperm into the water around them, and fertilization takes place when the male and female cells meet. But on land, this kind of fertilization is rare, because eggs and sperm quickly dry out. Instead, most land animals use a different method, called internal fertilization. The male and female pair up and mate, and the male inserts his sperm into his partner.

External fertilization
During the breeding season, male toads pair up with females. The male grips his partner using his strong front legs and is almost impossible to dislodge. When the two toads reach a pond, the female starts to lay her long string of eggs. As soon as the eggs begin to emerge, the male releases his sperm into the water, which ensures that the eggs are fertilized.

Eggs aboard
At the beginning of the breeding season, a female toad's body is swollen with several thousand eggs.

Tight hold
The male toad grips his partner with his front legs. To stop him from slipping off, he has special roughened pads on his thumbs.

Mating cats
The time that mating takes varies among animals. In some butterflies, mating can take several hours. In cats, however, it is over in a matter of minutes.

Fatal encounter
This female praying mantis is finishing off an unusual meal – her male partner. Female praying mantises are larger than the males. During mating, they sometimes eat their mates, starting with the head and working downward. Males often manage to avoid this gruesome fate, but if a male does lose his head, the rest of his body completes the mating process.

Hanging on
During mating, empid flies hang from a twig. The male grips the twig with his front legs, and uses his other four legs to grip his partner.

Shaping silk
The male uses the flat pads on his front legs to make the silken cocoon.

Small but strong
The male's legs are slender, but they are easily strong enough to carry the female's weight.

Clasping claws
Sharp claws give the male a good grip on his partner's body.

Hidden eggs
Once the egg cells have been fertilized, mating is over. The female flies off to lay her eggs.

Ovary

Anus

Ready to reproduce
When the male becomes an adult, sperm cells develop inside his abdomen.

Cells on the move
The male's sperm cells travel through a tube into the female's body.

Pairing up
The empid flies lock the tips of their abdomens, so that the male's sperm cells can enter the female's body. If the sperm cells were exposed to the air, they would dry out and die.

Internal fertilization
The sperm cells make their way into the female's oviducts, where they fertilize her egg cells.

Aerial hunters
Empid flies catch other insects in midair. Sharp eyesight helps them to dart after their prey.

Empid flies mating
Female empid flies are aggressive hunters, so males have to be careful about making their approach. In this species, the male gives the female a silk-covered snack, which keeps her occupied while he mates. In some related species, the males behave differently. They also give their partners a silk-wrapped "present," but instead of containing insects, their cocoons contain nothing but air!

Well-wrapped gift
This cocoon contains an aphid, securely wrapped by long strands of elastic silk. Silk is liquid when it is made, but it turns solid as it is squeezed out of the male's body.

A liquid diet
Empid flies use their sharp claws for catching other insects. They suck fluid from their prey and then throw away the dry remains.

Giants on the beach
The difference in size between male and female elephant seals is bigger than in any other mammal. Males can weigh up to 3 ton, about four or five times as much as their mates. During the breeding season, the largest males fight ferociously for a chance to mate. They roar loudly and inflate their trunklike noses, before ripping into their rivals with extremely sharp teeth. Successful males guard a piece of beach and assemble a "harem" of breeding females.

Extended families

The dry, dusty soil of East Africa is home to one of the world's strangest mammals – a wrinkly rodent called the naked mole rat. Mole rats not only look odd, they also breed in a very unusual way. Instead of pairing up to raise their young, they live in large family groups called colonies, and share the work involved in staying alive. In each colony, only one female, called the queen, produces young. The other members of the colony are called workers. They forage for food and look after the queen's offspring. Animals that live like this are called "eusocial" species.

Queen and workers

A queen naked mole rat is about 4 in (10 cm) long. She weighs about one and a half times as much as the workers, and usually has one or two male partners. Workers can be either male or female.

The royal chamber

Mole rats feed on plant roots, and live entirely underground in a network of burrows. At the heart of this network is a football-sized chamber where the queen mole rat gives birth to her young. She can have up to 12 pups in a litter, and they take a year to mature. Chemicals in the queen's urine stop the other mole rats from mating.

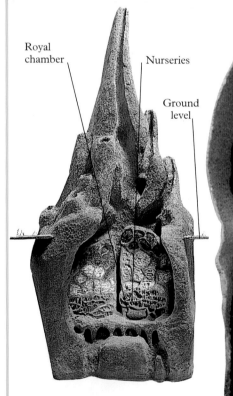

Royal chamber

Nurseries

Ground level

Termite mound

Termites live in giant family groups that can be over a million strong. In proportion to their size, they build the biggest homes of all land animals. Each nest contains a single queen who, trapped in a special cell, lays up to 30,000 eggs a day. She is much bigger than the workers, and can live for up to 70 years.

Tight fit
Although the queen weighs more than the workers, she is still slender enough to fit through the colony's narrow tunnels.

Living excavators
Workers use their feet to shovel soil backward when they dig.

Paper nests

Some wasps breed on their own, but many live in eusocial family groups. This wasp nest is built out of paper made from chewed-up wood fibers. It was started by a queen wasp and then expanded by her offspring. Wasps breed very quickly in summer, but in many species only the queen survives the winter.

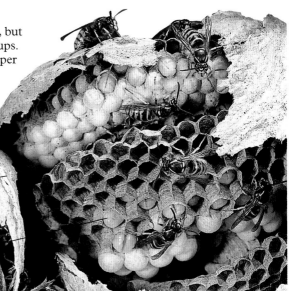

Insulation
Overlapping layers of paper keep the inside of the nest warm.

Nursery area
Wasp grubs grow up in cells inside the nest.

Dental chisels
Mole rats use their front teeth to dig and also to gnaw into their food. These teeth grow nonstop, which means they never wear down.

Trip to the toilet
Workers take the baby mole rats to the toilet burrow where they leave their droppings.

In touch
Naked mole rats do not have fur, but they do have extremely sensitive whiskers. Mole rats can also feel vibrations made by animals moving above.

Food supply
For their first few weeks, baby mole rats feed on the queen's milk. Later, workers bring them food.

Underground eyes
Mole rats can open their eyes, but because they live underground they rarely need to use them.

Eggs on board

California mountain kingsnakes entwined during mating

Most animals start life as a large single cell, or egg. In viviparous animals, eggs develop inside the mother, and the young are born alive. In oviparous animals, the eggs are laid at an earlier stage, and they complete their development outside the mother's body. Practically all the world's mammals have live young, while every single species of bird lays eggs. But in the world of reptiles, things are more complicated. Some reptiles bear live young. Others, such as the Burmese python, lay eggs that take several weeks to hatch. A few snakes and lizards reproduce in a different way. They are ovoviviparous, meaning that they keep their eggs in their bodies until they are ready to hatch.

Burmese python

This giant snake from Southeast Asia lays up to 60 leathery-shelled eggs each time it breeds. The eggs take about 14 weeks to develop inside the mother's body, and once they are laid they take a further eight weeks to hatch. During this time the mother wraps her body around the eggs, hiding them and keeping them warm.

Stretched out
The snake's internal organs are long and slender to fit in an elongated body.

Live birth

This European common lizard is giving birth to a family of live young. Live birth is common in snakes and lizards that live in cool parts of the world, where eggs would have difficulty developing. Thanks to this method of reproduction, the common lizard manages to survive and breed north of the Arctic Circle – a remarkable feat for a cold-blooded reptile.

Cryptic pattern
Disruptive markings help to break up the snake's outline.

Secret serpent
Superb camouflage conceals the python while it hunts for prey among the shadows of the forest floor.

Snakes are legless reptiles

Intestines
Before it can produce eggs, the python has to eat so that it can build up a store of fat.

Shriveled shell shows that egg is about to hatch

Main vein
This vein carries blood forward to the snake's heart.

Head tears through egg's leathery shell

Fat stores
Fat supplies the energy the snake needs to make its eggs.

Hatching out
Just before it hatches, the corn snake egg shrinks as the last of the yolk is used up. The snake then tears its way through the shell and crawls out. Hatching can take many hours, and the snake often hides in the shell if danger threatens.

Egg production
The eggs are formed in the ovaries by clusters of cells called follicles.

Ovulation
During ovulation, the egg cells or ova are shed from the ovaries into the oviduct.

Kidney
The python's kidneys are long and slender. Instead of being side by side, as in most animals, one is behind the other.

Feeding time
Young snakes are ready to hunt within hours of hatching.

Fertilization
The eggs are fertilized in the oviduct before their shells develop.

Developing egg
The growth of the embryo is entirely dependent on yolk in the egg.

Ready to lay
Muscles push each egg out of an opening called the cloaca.

Moving coils
Once the eggs have been laid, the snake shuffles them with her body to catch the early morning sunshine.

Nothing by mouth
In many species, the female does not eat while she is holding eggs.

Skin change
The skin of female snakes may darken during the breeding season.

Laying eggs

On warm summer nights, female grasshoppers search for a patch of sandy ground. They carefully dig into it with their abdomens and slowly lay batches of eggs. Grasshoppers, like many other animals, take care when laying their eggs. Some bury them in the ground or fasten them to plants, while others lay them in specially constructed nests. Nest makers often look after their eggs until they hatch. However, other egg layers abandon them once they have been laid.

Eggs on the beach
Under the cover of darkness, oceangoing turtles crawl onto sandy beaches to lay their eggs. They use their back flippers to excavate a hole and then slowly drop their eggs into it.

Eggs underground
Many species of grasshopper bury their eggs in the ground. This keeps the eggs moist and protects them from hungry animals. During egg laying, the female grasshopper's abdomen can stretch up to three times its normal length and tunnel into the ground.

Sealed in
Once the eggs have been laid, the female closes up the hole and often seals it with quick-drying foam.

Elastic abdomen
The abdomen is covered by hard plates that are connected by softer skin. This skin stretches when the female digs downward.

Digging down
Small flaps at the end of the abdomen open and close as she digs, forcing a hole through the ground.

Egg production
Eggs form in two rows of ovaries inside the grasshopper's abdomen.

Oviduct

Anus

Multiple batches
Some grasshoppers lay only a few eggs, but others lay up to 50 in a batch.

Filled with froth
Grasshoppers and locusts often produce froth when they lay their eggs. The froth helps keep the eggs moist.

Tuning in
A grasshopper's ears are on the sides of its abdomen.

Reluctant fliers
Most grasshoppers have wings, but they usually move around on their legs.

Eggs under guard
This female harlequin bug is standing guard over her brightly colored eggs. Compared to most insects, bugs are unusually careful parents. Some water bugs carry their eggs on their backs.

On the alert
Good eyesight warns grasshoppers of approaching danger, but when a female is laying eggs she has difficulty making an escape.

Holding steady
Strong claws help to anchor the grasshopper while she digs her way into the ground.

Courtship calls
Most grasshoppers find their partner by sound. Males rub their hindlegs against their bodies, making a call that attracts the females.

Frog embrace
The male frog clasps the female and fertilizes the eggs as she lays them.

Egg string
Toads lay strings of eggs.

Finding the spot
Some butterflies and moths drop their eggs from the air, but most – such as this Malay lacewing butterfly – carefully search out suitable food plants, and then cement their eggs in position. When the caterpillars emerge from the eggs, they will have plenty of food to eat.

Laying underwater
Frogs and toads lay eggs underwater. A female common toad can lay up to 4,000 eggs. She lays them in long strings, which she wraps around underwater plants. As soon as the eggs leave her body, the male fertilizes them. Frogs can lay as many as 20,000 eggs in one clump.

Eggs on stalks
Insect eggs make an easy meal for small animals, and many get eaten before they have a chance to hatch. Lacewings get around this problem by laying their eggs on stalks. The stalks are harder for predators to reach.

Growth in the egg

After it has been fertilized, an egg begins to develop. Its original cell divides into two, and the new cells then divide again. Many more divisions quickly follow, as the new cells begin to rearrange themselves and develop in different ways. Bit by bit, a young animal, or embryo, starts to take shape. In a frog's egg, these remarkable changes can be seen from outside, because the jelly around the egg is transparent. In a bird's egg, an embryo develops into a fully feathered chick, hidden away by the shell.

Popping out
Young birds break their way out of their eggs, but lice, such as this head louse, have a different way of hatching. They push against the top end of the egg case, or nit, opening a special lid that lets them out. Many other insects hatch by eating their way through their shells.

Chalaza (spiral cord) Embryonic disc Air sac

Day one
By the time the egg is laid, it already contains several thousand cells. They form a small patch called an embryonic disk that lies on the surface of the yolk.

Position of heart Head Air sac
Network of blood vessels

Day three
The embryonic disk has developed into an embryo. Its heart pumps blood through a network of blood vessels. The blood collects food from the yolk and carries it to the embryo.

Wraparound membrane
The chorion contains blood vessels that collect oxygen seeping into the egg.

Tight fit
The chick fills the whole egg. The yolk has been completely used up.

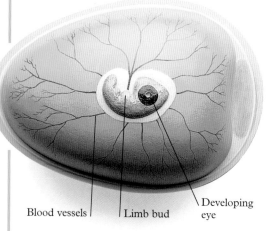

Blood vessels Limb bud Developing eye

Day seven
The embryo is now growing fast. Its eyes are developing, and it also has small limb buds that will grow into legs and wings. Oxygen from the air seeps through tiny pores in the shell and is carried to the embryo by blood vessels.

How a chicken's egg develops
Like most other birds, chickens incubate their eggs, sitting on them to keep them warm. In chickens, incubation does not start until the last egg has been laid, but from then on it has to continue nonstop or the chicks will die. Chicken eggs contain a large amount of yolk. This provides enough food for the embryos to turn into well developed chicks.

Allantois containing chick's waste Fluid-filled space Air sac

Day 12
The embryo's limb buds are now much bigger, and its head and beak are taking shape. A special sac called the allantois is filling with the chick's waste. Without this sac, the chick would be poisoned.

Waste sac
The allantois collects the chick's waste so that it is not poisoned inside the shell.

Day 20
The chick has just one more day to go before it hatches. It has used up all the food in the yolk and has grown a complete covering of feathers. The chick will hatch by pecking at the shell until it breaks.

Rolling around

This nesting oystercatcher is about to use her beak to rearrange her eggs. By doing this, she makes sure that all the eggs stay at an even temperature. When she moves an egg, the yolk inside turns to keep the embryo facing upward.

Taking turns

In many birds the female takes charge of incubating the eggs. Ostriches are different. Several females often lay in the same nest, and they sometimes sit on the nest during the day. At night, the male takes over incubation.

Eye
Unlike many nesting birds, a chick can see as soon as it hatches.

Ready to run
The chick's legs are fully developed so that it can run to keep up with its mother.

Easy exit
The shell's curved shape makes it easier to break from the inside than the outside.

Egg tooth
The chick uses this hard bump near the tip of its beak to help it chip through the shell.

Air supply
A few hours before hatching, the chick breaks into the air sac and starts to breathe air for the first time.

Packed flat
The chick's feathers lie flat inside the egg, but they soon dry out and fluff up when it hatches.

Parasite parents

Hidden away inside another animal's intestines, a tapeworm lives in a world that is full of food. It never has to move around to eat, and it never has to fight off any enemies. Instead, it can put all its energy into the extremely important task of making millions and millions of eggs. Parasites are extremely common in the animal kingdom. All of them live on or inside other animals' bodies, and all of them have to find some way to spread. Parasites like the tapeworm produce as many eggs or young as possible to increase the chances that at least a few will manage to find new hosts. Tapeworms are passed to new hosts through infected meat.

Copepods are parasites that feed on sharks' skin

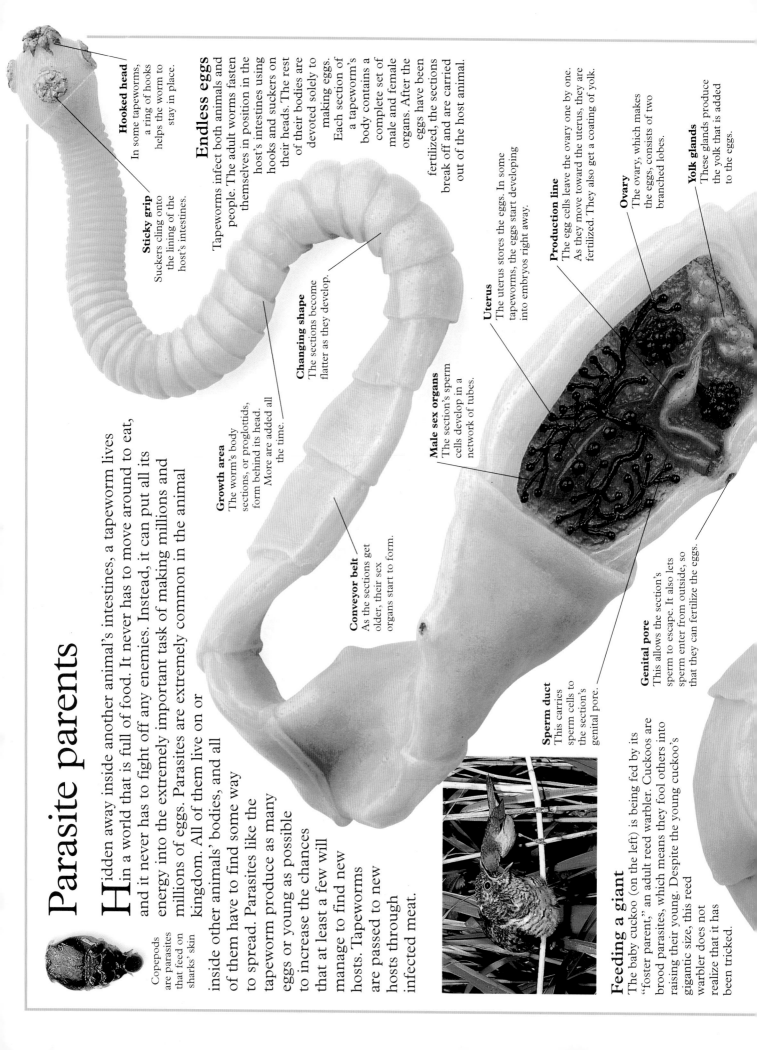

Hooked head
In some tapeworms, a ring of hooks helps the worm to stay in place.

Sticky grip
Suckers cling onto the lining of the host's intestines.

Endless eggs
Tapeworms infect both animals and people. The adult worms fasten themselves in position in the host's intestines using hooks and suckers on their heads. The rest of their bodies are devoted solely to making eggs. Each section of a tapeworm's body contains a complete set of male and female organs. After the eggs have been fertilized, the sections break off and are carried out of the host animal.

Changing shape
The sections become flatter as they develop.

Growth area
The worm's body sections, or proglottids, form behind its head. More are added all the time.

Conveyor belt
As the sections get older, their sex organs start to form.

Male sex organs
The section's sperm cells develop in a network of tubes.

Uterus
The uterus stores the eggs. In some tapeworms, the eggs start developing into embryos right away.

Production line
The egg cells leave the ovary one by one. As they move toward the uterus, they are fertilized. They also get a coating of yolk.

Ovary
The ovary, which makes the eggs, consists of two branched lobes.

Yolk glands
These glands produce the yolk that is added to the eggs.

Sperm duct
This carries sperm cells to the section's genital pore.

Genital pore
This allows the section's sperm to escape. It also lets sperm enter from outside, so that they can fertilize the eggs.

Feeding a giant
The baby cuckoo (on the left) is being fed by its "foster parent," an adult reed warbler. Cuckoos are brood parasites, which means they fool others into raising their young. Despite the young cuckoo's gigantic size, this reed warbler does not realize that it has been tricked.

Living ribbon
A tapeworm's body can be over 33 ft (10 m) long, but is rarely more than 0.4 in (1 cm) wide.

Eaten alive
Clusters of tiny silk cocoons show that this caterpillar has been attacked by parasitic insects. The tiny braconid wasp injects its eggs into the caterpillar. When the grubs hatch, they eat their host.

Parasitic partners
In the sea's greatest depths, finding a partner can be a problem. Angler fish solve this in a remarkable way. The males are much smaller than the females, and when they find a mate, they fasten themselves to her side. From then on they live parasitically, fertilizing the female's eggs but relying on her for food.

Absorbing food
Tapeworms do not have mouths or digestive systems of their own. Instead, they absorb food substances from their hosts directly through the surface of their bodies.

Complex combinations
A section can fertilize its own eggs, or its eggs can be fertilized by sperm from other sections – either from the same tapeworm, or from one nearby.

Taking turns
In neighboring sections, the sex organs are arranged in opposite directions. This means that the genital pores are also arranged on alternating sides.

Doubled up
The ichneumon swings its ovipositor forward to push it into the sand.

Ichneumon wasp about to lay eggs in ground

The ovipositor can be over 1 in (2.5 cm) long

Killer driller
Like a doctor making an injection, a female ichneumon wasp slides her ovipositor into the sand. Gliding it carefully downward, she will eventually make contact with an insect grub that she has sensed hiding beneath the surface. She will then lay a single egg next to the grub, leaving it to hatch and eat its host. Ichneumons find their victims mainly by smell and through the sensitive tips of their ovipositors.

Fully packed
A ripe section can contain about 100,000 eggs. When it nears the end of the animal, the section breaks away.

Into the world
The eggs are swept out of the host's body. They only hatch if they are eaten by another animal.

Egg-laying mammals

There are 4,000 species of mammals in the world, and almost all of them give birth to live young. In Australia and New Guinea, however, there are three remarkable animals known as monotremes. They have warm blood and fur, and feed their young milk like other mammals. But instead of giving birth to live young, they lay tiny eggs. Two species of monotremes, called echidnas or spiny anteaters, are covered in sharp quills. The female has a pouch in which she incubates a single egg. The third species, the duck-billed platypus, does not have a pouch. Instead, the female incubates her eggs in a waterside burrow.

Laid back
This female echidna is lying on her back, showing her pouch. It is formed by two flaps of swollen skin that run lengthwise underneath her body. After a young echidna hatches, it has to crawl toward the front of the pouch to reach its mother's milk.

Echidna egg
An echidna's egg is the size of a small grape. It has a leathery shell and fits into a pocket at the rear end of the mother's pouch. The short-nosed echidna's egg takes about 11 days to hatch.

Newly hatched
This baby echidna is less than 0.6 in (15 mm) long. Although it is poorly developed, its stubby front legs already have tiny claws for gripping its mother's fur. After hatching it clambers forward for its first meal of milk.

Fur is sparser around edge of the pouch

Soft fur
The skin on an echidna's underside does not have spines. It is covered with soft fur.

Ant-proof underside
Tough skin protects the echidna from biting ants that often swarm over it as it feeds.

Muscle pouch
Instead of being bag-shaped, the echidna's pouch is formed by two muscles that run along its underside.

Mammal with a beak
As well as laying eggs, the duck-billed platypus has two other extraordinary features. Its mouth is shaped like a duck's beak, and the males have poisonous claws. It uses its beak to forage for small animals underwater, and males probably use their poison claws to fend off rivals. When the first stuffed platypus reached Europe, scientists were so suspicious of it that they decided it was a hoax.

Fast feeder
This young echidna is just starting to grow its spines, and it will soon leave its mother's pouch.

Digging down
Echidnas feed on ants and other small insects. They claw open ants' nests and lap them up with their tongues. If an echidna senses danger, it either stands absolutely still or it rapidly burrows into the ground.

Sharp quills set in soft fur

Upside down
Here the female is lying on her back with her baby above her.

Head hold
The muscular edges of the pouch help keep the baby echidna in place.

Hanging on
When newly hatched, the baby's claws are so small that they can cling to individual hairs. Later on, they grip the mother's skin.

Milk patch
The baby echidna quickly sucks up milk as it oozes onto the surface of the pouch.

Milk pores
The mammary glands empty into pores in the milk pouch.

Mammary glands
Several hundred glands produce a supply of highly nutritious milk.

Feeding time
With its head pressed inside mother's pouch, this young echidna – or "puggle" – is busily lapping up a meal of milk. Unlike other mammals, female echidnas do not have teats. Instead, the milk oozes out into an area called the milk patch, and the baby echidna sucks it up. A young short-nosed echidna stays in its mother's pouch for about 60 days. This one is about 45 days old and is nearly too big to fit inside.

Making clones

In spring and early summer, when plants are growing fast, tiny sap-sucking insects called aphids have all the food they can possibly eat. To make the most of this feast, they reproduce by parthenogenesis, or "virgin birth." During this process, each female aphid gives birth without having to mate and is soon surrounded by dozens of babies. The young aphids are clones, which means they are identical to each other in every way. At the end of summer, aphids reproduce by mating and laying eggs.

Production line birth
Aphids that are born live develop from unfertilized eggs inside the mother's body.

Easy pickings
This adult ladybug is munching its favorite food – a young aphid. Aphids move slowly and have few defenses, so ladybugs can eat dozens of them a day. However, aphids make up for this by reproducing much faster than their enemies can eat them.

Backward exit
Unlike most young animals, baby aphids are born backward, so their heads emerge last.

Liquid meal
The mother's digestive system is full of sugary plant sap.

Staying together
The young aphids cluster together on the soft tips of plant stems.

Fast breeder

Every day a female aphid can give birth to as many as six young. In spring and early summer, the young are always female. Several all-female generations follow each other, but in late summer males begin to appear. Females then mate with the males and lay eggs.

Cloning lizards

Several kinds of whiptail lizards from North America can reproduce by "virgin birth." However, rather than give birth to live young like aphids, whiptail lizards lay eggs. The babies are always female; males are unknown.

Piercing mouthpart

Stuck in
Aphids feed by piercing plant stems with their sharp mouthparts. These fold back when not in use.

Inside story

Most of the world's mammals spend their early life in the safest place of all – inside their mother's body. Tucked away in a chamber called the uterus, or womb, they are kept warm and well fed and are hidden away from their natural enemies. Mammals that develop in this way are called "placentals," because their young are nourished in a special way. Each embryo grows a spongy organ called a placenta, which collects nutrients and oxygen from the mother's blood. The smallest placental mammals are ready to be born in less than 12 days. Larger ones, such as gorillas, stay inside their mother for many months.

Giving birth

This female cat is giving birth to a family of kittens. As each kitten emerges, the mother licks away the membranes that surround it. The kitten is then able to take its first breath. The mother also chews through the umbilical cord, which connects the kitten to its placenta, and eats the placenta itself. This natural recycling helps to keep the kittens clean and provides the mother with a useful meal.

Expectant mother

A female gorilla usually gives birth every three or four years. She normally has a single baby, which takes just over eight months to develop. Although she weighs about twice as much as the average woman, her babies are smaller than human ones.

The way out
The mother's birth canal, or vagina, stretches wide open to let the baby gorilla pass through.

Forced exit
The uterus is surrounded by strong muscles. When the baby is born, the muscles contract to force it out.

Safe storage
In the uterus, the young gorilla floats in a pool of special fluid. This protects it from sudden jolts as the mother moves.

Umbilical cord
The umbilical cord transfers food and oxygen from the placenta to the baby.

Changing shape
As the baby develops, it takes up more space in the mother's abdomen. The mother's intestines shift forward to let the uterus expand.

Placenta

Feeding time

Here a family of puppies are suckling their mother's milk. Making milk for her pups enables the mother to go off to find food for herself without having to bring it back. As the pups develop, the mother's behavior changes, and she shares her food with her young.

Newborn fox cubs cannot see or hear.

At two weeks old the cub's eyes are open and it can see.

Six week old fox cub

Eight week old fox cub

At ten weeks old the fox cub is almost independent.

Growing up

Like many newly born mammals, a young fox cub is completely helpless. It relies on its mother for food and protection. However, fox cubs soon grow up. Within four weeks they are playing with their brothers and sisters, and within eight weeks they are eating solid food. Because young mammals grow up close to their mothers, they have lots of opportunities to learn. Fox clubs find out about hunting by watching their mothers at work.

Motherly embrace
Female gorillas often use their arms both to cradle their young and to protect them if anything dangerous comes too close.

Mobile homes

Marsupial frog carries tadpoles in a pouch

Many animals protect their eggs by making nests. However, a number of animals have a different way of keeping their eggs safe. After the eggs have been laid, one of the parents picks them up and carries them until they hatch. These living egg-carriers include insects, spiders, crustaceans, and frogs, but the strangest of all is the Surinam toad. In this species, as the female lays her eggs in the water, the male fastens them in place on her back. Once the eggs are in position, a special layer of spongy skin grows up around them and completely hides them while they develop. After many weeks, the young break out of their mobile home. Instead of emerging as tadpoles, like most young amphibians, they are released as tiny toads.

Onboard development
After each egg hatches, a tadpole develops inside the chamber.

Getting oxygen
During their development, the tadpoles absorb oxygen through their skins and tails.

Breakout
The young emerge by pushing open the lid on their chambers. Any part of their body can come first.

Locked inside
A tough lid covers each egg and protects it as it develops.

Separate quarters
Each egg becomes surrounded by skin, forming a chamber on the toad's back.

Fully formed
The newly emerged toads are like miniature versions of their parents.

Spongy skin
The spongy layer develops within hours of mating and egg laying. It remains until the tadpoles have emerged.

Temporarily grounded
In some giant water bugs, the female cements the eggs onto her partner's wings, and he carries them until they hatch. Water bugs are strong flyers, but a male with eggs cannot use his wings.

Surinam toad
This bizarre-looking amphibian lives in murky streams in tropical South America. Just before the female is ready to lay her eggs, the male grips her by the waist. The pair then carry out a series of underwater somersaults, with the female laying eggs while she is upside down. Using his back legs and body, the male presses the eggs onto the female's back, and they later become embedded in her swollen skin.

34

Powerful kick
The female uses her large, webbed hind feet to push herself to the surface during her egg-laying somersaults.

Staying aboard
Female spiders often carry their eggs in special silk cocoons. After the spiderlings hatch, they sometimes stay aboard their mother for several days until they are big enough to molt (shed their skins). This female meadow spider has caught a fly. While she feeds, her tiny offspring cling to the surface of her abdomen.

Powerful claw

Antennae

Stalked eye

Cryptic color
The toad's dull colors camouflage it as it rests on the bottom of streams.

Ready to run
If the crab is in danger, it can lift the egg mass off of the ground, allowing it to scuttle away.

Folded away
The eggs are held in place by the short abdomen at the back of its body.

Midwife toad is found in western Europe

Male midwives
When a female midwife toad lays her string of eggs, the male winds them around his back legs. He then carries the eggs for about a month, visiting pools and puddles to keep them moist. Just before the eggs are ready to hatch, the male places them in a suitable pool, and the tadpoles wriggle away into the water.

Backpack
The male carries a string of up to 60 eggs.

Tied up
The string of eggs are wrapped around the toad's legs.

Eggs underneath
Like many other crustaceans, the female velvet crab carries her eggs beneath her body. She produces thousands of eggs each time she breeds and packs the eggs into a spongy mass between her back legs. Her abdomen holds the eggs in place. Velvet crab eggs hatch out to produce tiny larvae that drift away in the water. It is several weeks before they develop into crabs.

Caring parents

For the first days or weeks of life, baby animals are often in danger. They are small and inexperienced, which makes them easy prey. However, their chances of survival are greatly increased if they are looked after by their parents. Parent animals care for their young in many different ways. Some of them stand guard over their young and attack anything that comes too close. Many build special nests or dens, where their young are hidden from predators and protected from the weather outside. Some extraordinary fish go further than this. They use their bodies as living shelters and let their young swim aboard when danger threatens.

Fatherly care
Female seahorses place their newly laid eggs into a special pouch on the front of the male's body. The male incubates the young and protects them when they are newly hatched. When the young are ready to leave the pouch, the male looks as if he is giving birth.

Tail clings to underwater plants

Going out
When the coast is clear, the mother fish closes her gill covers, pumping the young out of her mouth.

Pregnant pouch
The male's pouch swells up during the breeding season. It has a small opening that receives the eggs.

Shoal of young fish

Safely stowed
The mother's mouth provides enough room for dozens of young.

Night shelter
As they get older, the young fish spend more time outside. For the first month, they still return to their mother's mouth at night.

Time to eat
For the first few days, the young fish live on yolk from their eggs. After this they have to leave their mother's mouth to feed.

Hitching a lift
Cygnets (young swans) often clamber aboard their parents' backs when danger threatens or when they need to rest. Cygnets usually climb off if their parents reach underwater to feed, but other young water birds, such as grebes, cling to their parents even when they dive.

Mobile mouthful
The yellow-banded cichlid is one of many mouthbrooding fish that live in African lakes and rivers. After the fish has laid her eggs, she scoops them up in her mouth. The eggs hatch out, and the young fish stay in her mouth until they are big enough to venture outside.

On the alert

In most mammals, the mother's instinct to look after her young is extremely strong. This female wild boar is listening for any sounds that might spell danger for her litter of striped piglets. If any other animal comes too close, she will not hesitate to launch an attack.

Carried to water

Using her huge jaws, a female crocodile gently carries her newly hatched young to water. Her nest may contain over 50 eggs, so it takes several trips to complete the job.

Fish mates
Cichlids often stay with their mates after they have raised their young.

Lake dweller
This cichlid is found in Africa's Lake Malawi.

Oxygen supply
The mother pumps water through her gills, keeping up a steady flow that provides her young with oxygen.

Life in a pouch

Virginia opossum

When the first European settlers reached Australia, they were amazed by the animals they found there. Instead of embryos developing inside the womb as in placental mammals (pp. 32–33), Australia's native mammals give birth to tiny young and then raise them in a pouch. Mammals like these are called "marsupials." The pouch resembles a big bag, and is located just below the mother's chest. As well as protecting the young, it houses nipples from which they can feed. Marsupials are much less common than placental mammals, but they are still very well adapted for survival. A female wallaby or kangaroo can have both a newly born and a well-grown baby, or joey, feeding from her pouch at the same time. This allows her to nurture two generations of young at once.

1 To prepare for the birth, the mother licks a clear path through her fur for the joey to follow.

2 Joeys are born at a very early stage of their development. This joey is about 0.75 in (2 cm) long, and weighs less than 0.2 oz (5 g). Only its front legs work, and it uses these to haul itself on the marathon journey from the birth canal to the pouch's opening.

3 Once in the pouch, the joey fastens its mouth to one of its mother's nipples. For the next four months, it will not leave the pouch, growing all the time.

Feeding station
The nipple grows in step with the joey, and eventually becomes about 4 in (10 cm) long.

Ready for use
A newly born joey fastens itself to one of the smallest nipples.

Plenty to spare
A kangaroo's pouch usually contains four nipples.

Stepping out
After developing in the pouch, a young kangaroo or wallaby begins to try life outside. It still reaches into the pouch to drink milk and climbs back inside if danger threatens. Meanwhile, a new joey starts to grow inside the pouch.

Adult wallaby

This way around
Kangaroos and wallabies have forward-facing pouches.

Young wallaby

Embryos in reserve
Embryos are stored until they are needed. A new embryo starts to develop when a joey is about to leave the pouch.

Return trip
The joey suckles milk for up to a year after leaving the pouch.

Tight grip
A young koala spends six months in its mother's pouch and then climbs out and clings onto her back. The koala's pouch has a narrow entrance to stop the young from falling out.

Changing back

After a joey has left the pouch, the nipple it used shrinks to its former size.

Struggle for survival

The Virginia opossum is found in North America. It often gives birth to more than 20 young, but since it has only 13 nipples some of them soon die. The opossum's pouch is small, and the surviving young quickly get too big to fit inside. Instead, they dangle beneath their mother as she climbs in trees.

Opossums clinging to their mother

Adult opossum

Keeping warm

The skin inside the pouch is almost bare of fur to let the mother's body warmth reach the joey.

Slow coat

The joey's fur starts to grow when it is about eight weeks old.

Putting on weight

By the time it is ready to leave the pouch, the joey will have increased to over 200 times its original weight.

4 The joey is now about six weeks old. For most of its time in the pouch, it will stay permanently fastened to one of its mother's nipples. Once the joey starts to suckle, the nipple expands so that the joey is difficult to dislodge. The consistency of the mother's milk gradually changes as the joey grows, providing it with all the different nutrients that it needs to develop.

Changing shape

Tadpole – the larva of a frog

All animals change as they grow up. In some animals the young start life looking similar to their parents. But in others the changes are far-reaching, and the animal's body is entirely transformed. This drastic change of shape is called metamorphosis. It allows the adult and the young to live in totally different ways from each other. They can perform different roles, eat different types of food, and inhabit different environments. Apart from fish and amphibians, few vertebrates undergo metamorphosis. However, it is very common in less complex creatures – particularly in animals that spend their lives in water.

Live-in larva
A larva is any young animal that changes shape completely as it grows up. This is the larva of a caddis fly, an insect that spends the first part of its life in water. Caddis fly larvae protect themselves from being eaten by other water animals by constructing tubular cases out of sand grains, tiny sticks, shells, and blades of grass.

First antenna

Central naupliar eye

Carapace (hard shield)

Frontal horn

Mouthparts

Midgut

Eye

Carapace

Setae

First antenna

1 After weeks adrift at sea, the nauplius larva of a barnacle changes into a cyprid larva. Unlike the nauplius larva, the cyprid larva does not feed.

First antenna

Cement gland

Setae

2 If the cyprid larva settles on a suitable rock, it begins to change into an adult. First, it cements itself in position.

Chalky plates

3 The larva becomes enclosed by chalky plates. Its "feet" now point upward, so they can be used to collect food.

Setae | Mouth

Life adrift
Unless you are a marine biologist, you might have trouble identifying this strange-looking animal. Amazingly, it is the "nauplius" larva of a barnacle – an animal that spends its adult life fastened in one place. In contrast, barnacle larvae drift about in the sea.

Fringed setae (legs)

Tail

Settling down
Like barnacles, crabs spend the first part of their lives as larvae that drift in the sea. A young crab larva, called a zoea, has long spines and feathery legs. It changes into a megalopa larva which settles on the sea floor. This turns into a miniature adult crab.

Megalopa larva

Shaped for strength
The barnacle's plates fit together to form a conical shape – ideal for withstanding the battering of the waves.

Adult box crab

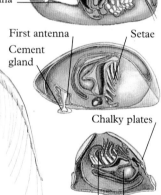

Adult barnacle

After it has completed its metamorphosis, an adult barnacle spends the rest of its life firmly fastened to a piece of rock. Its body is surrounded by a set of armored plates, and at low tide it shuts itself in to avoid drying out. It feeds by filtering tiny particles of food from the water.

Extra-large penis enables barnacle to fertilize other barnacles

Sieving food
Cirri, or fringed feeding legs, are used to catch tiny animals and particles of food.

Swallowtails lay their eggs singly on suitable foodplants

Caterpillar uses its jaws to eat its way out of the egg

Caterpillar feeds voraciously and quickly grows

Caterpillar turns into a pupa

Butterfly metamorphosis

A caterpillar is the larva of a butterfly or moth. It changes shape suddenly during a resting stage called a pupa. In this part of its life cycle, the caterpillar's body is broken down and completely rearranged.

Adult butterfly emerges from pupal case

Egg point
This opening sheds the barnacle's eggs into its mantle cavity.

Mouth
The cirri place food into the barnacle's mouth.

Swallowtail butterfly

Oviduct
This tube carries the eggs from the ovary toward the oviduct opening.

Egg mass
The eggs collect inside the mantle cavity and are fertilized by a neighboring barnacle.

Ovary
This makes the barnacle's eggs. The eggs move into the mantle cavity, where they are fertilized. They hatch out as nauplius larvae and drift away.

41

Glossary

Barnacle larva

Adult barnacle

A

Allantois
A special baglike membrane attached to an embryo. It collects waste and sometimes helps to gather oxygen.

Asexual reproduction
Any kind of reproduction that involves only a one parent.

B

Breeding season
The part of an animal's life when it is able to breed. Many animals have just one breeding season a year.

Budding
A kind of reproduction in which young animals grow from buds on their parents.

C

Chorion
The outer covering of an embryo.

Clone
A collection of identical living things that come from the same parent and share exactly the same genes.

Courtship
A special kind of behavior used by animals to attract a mate.

E

Egg cell
A special female cell that can produce a new animal. To develop, egg cells (ova) usually have to be fertilized by sperm.

Embryo
A young animal in the early stages of development.

Embryonic disk
The patch of cells in a bird's egg that develops into a young bird.

Eusocial species
A species that lives in large family groups, known as colonies. In each colony, only one female reproduces. She is known as the queen.

F

Fertilization
The joining together of a male and a female cell (sperm and egg) to produce a new living thing.

Follicle
A small cluster of cells that surrounds an egg cell. Follicles are found in female organs called ovaries.

Grasshopper laying eggs

G

Genes
The chemical instructions that make living things work.

H

Hatching
Breaking out of an egg. Some animals hatch by eating their way out, but other animals have to break or tear open the shell of the egg.

Hermaphrodite
Any animal (or plant) that has both male and female reproductive organs.

I

Incubate
To sit on eggs. Incubation keeps eggs warm and enables them to develop.

Internal fertilization
Fertilization that takes place inside the mother's body.

L

Larva
A young animal that develops by changing shape.

M

Mammary gland
A gland in female mammals that produces milk.

Marsupial
A mammal that raises its young in a pouch. The young are born while their development is still at an early stage.

Metamorphosis
A complete change in body shape that takes place as some animals develop.

Milk
A liquid food made by female mammals for their young.

Monotreme
A mammal that reproduces by laying eggs. Monotremes are found only in Australia and New Guinea.

N

Nest
Any kind of shelter made by animals to protect themselves or their eggs and young from predators and the weather.

Nipple
The place where young mammals suckle milk from their mother. Also known as a teat.

Fiddler crab

O

Ovary
In female animals, the reproductive organ that makes egg cells, or ova.

Oviduct
A tube that carries ova out of a female animal's ovaries.

Oviparous
A word used for any animal that reproduces by laying eggs.

Ovoviviparous
Animals that lay their eggs at the moment that they are ready to hatch.

Ovipositor
A tubelike organ that some female animals use when laying eggs.

P

Parthenogenesis
Reproduction using egg cells that do not need to be fertilized.

Penis
The external organ used by male animals to introduce sperm cells into the female's body.

Pouch
In marsupials, a special chamber on the outside of the mother's body that is used to house the developing young.

Placenta
A spongy pad attached to an embryo animal that collects food and oxygen from its mother.

Pregnancy
The period of time that a female animal carries her unborn young inside her body.

S

Sexual reproduction
Reproduction that involves a male and a female parent, or more rarely, parents that are both sexes at once.

Spermatophore
A package containing sperm cells.

Sperm cell
A special kind of male cell that fertilizes egg cells to create a new animal.

Baby kangaroo suckling in a pouch

U

Umbilical cord
A cord that connects an embryo to a placenta. It carries food to the embryo from its mother and carries away waste.

Uterus
The organ inside female mammals that protects developing young.

V

Vagina
The channel that connects a female mammal's uterus to the outside.

Viviparous
A word used to describe animals that give birth to live young.

Y

Yolk
The nutritious substance inside an egg that supplies a developing animal with food.

Burmese python laying egg

Index

Acknowledgments

The publisher would like to thank:
Phil Manning, University of Sheffield,
and Mark O'Shea for advice. Maggie
Tingle for design assistance. Jayne
Parsons and Miranda Smith for
proofreading. Marion Dent for the
index. Special thanks to Robert
Graham for his excellent research.

Artwork: Dominic Zwemmer

Jacket design: Sophia Tampakopoulos

Additional photography: Jane
Burton, Steve Gorton, Frank

Greenaway, Kim Taylor, Harry Taylor,
Mike Linley, and Dave King.

Picture Credits:
Key: t=top; b=below; c= center; l=left;
r=right

Kiyokazu Agata @ Himeji Institute of
Technology 11bc;
Aquila Photographic: Les Baker
26cl;
Ardea London Ltd: John Clegg 10cl;
Pascal Goetgheluck 17cl; Valerie Taylor
24tr;
Bruce Coleman: Fred Bruemmer

23tr; Dr.Eckart Pott 14bl; Andrew
J.Purcell 14cl; Kevin Rushby 25bl; Kim
Taylor 19tr;
Frank Lane Picture Agency: K.
Maslowski 3tr; P Perry 36bc; Roger
Tidman 12clb; Chris Mattison: 20cl,
31tr;
Nature Focus: Rismac 28cl, clb, tr;
**Natural History Photographic
Agency:** A.N.T. 2br; Ashod Francis
Papazian 40bc; Peter Parks 40cb; John
Shaw 3cr; Norbert Wu 27br;
Oxford Scientific Films: Animals,
Animals/ Ralph Reinhold 12tr; G.I.
Bernard 11cb; Scott Camazine/M.

Marchetorre 11tr; Wolfgang
Lummer/Okapia 37tr; Harold
Taylor/Abipp 30cl; Konrad Wothe
17cl; David Parker/Elizabeth Parker-
Cook: 28bl;
Planet Earth Pictures: Geoff du Feu
15tl; Roger de la Harpe 37tl; Stephen
P. Hopkin 8clb, 10br; 14tr W.B.Irwin
25br; Ken Lucas 34bl;
Premaphotos Wildlife: K.G.
Preston-Mafham 24tr, 27cr;
Science Photo Library: J.C. Revy
22tr;
Warren Photographic: Jane Burton
15tc; Kim Taylor 35tc.